AF619997

# Thoughts in a Small Room

## An Exercise in Poetic License

By Christopher Brown

# PREFACE

This little book is a collection of poems and such which I wrote during my first months in BallyCara Hostel. I had to move in to the Hostel as it became clear that I could no longer live safely at home due to serious falls risks.

Organising the various poems into categories was my original thought but on reflection I decided to leave them in the order pretty much that I penned them. No inference should be drawn as to my state of mind for each one. For instance the poem about Brunswick green occurred while eating lunch and watching the painters paint over that colour guttering around the Hostel.

Any mistakes are mine of course though one has to allow for poetic license which I claim in each and every applicable instance.

I dedicate this effort to my Darling Wife Barbara.

Thanks also to Chris, Ian, Leif, Greg, Colin, Keith, Cam and many more who bring light into my life.

November 2018 BallyCara Village

Contents

## The Nursing Home

I've had to move into a Nursing Home
I can no longer walk or stand
And if I try to do it, the floor is where I'll land.

It's not as bad as all that
I get three square meals a day
Most of its delicious - I think that's all I'll say.

My room is fairly self-contained
I try not to be a fuzzer
Cos' I can cause a ruckus, with my handy little buzzer

They have a stand up hoisty thing
To move me round about
As I dangle in the air, trying hard not to shout.

They move me to the toilet
The electric chairs my chum
It lifts me up into the air so they can wipe my bum.

My trusty wheelchair is a boon
You can see me whiz about
Sometimes I speeds a little which makes the helpers shout.

There's stuff to keep us busy
There's stuff to keep us sane
I just occasionally remind them all I really have a brain.

Everyone is lovely
Which helps to make it nice
And I return the compliments which helps to melt the ice.

I am so thankful for my lot
It could be so much worse
So I will let some steam off with a modicum of verse.
!
So to all my very faithful friends
It is so nice to see ya.
Keep calling in to share my days, you are my hallelujah!

## Beetroot

My lunch turned up today, I will relate
With a lump of reddish stuff reposing on my plate.

Oh! I really do detest you, you get right up my snoot
I have always been that way when confronted by beetroot!

There's many that do like the stuff strange as it may seem
But I'm not one, no never, the sight just makes me scream.

Now here's a wonder I confess when considering stuff so hellish
I happen contradictably being partial to beetroot relish!

## Reflections on a lake in northern Italy

Stunning Lake Garda is close to the foothills of the Alps.
On the southern shore is a beautiful peninsular, Sirmione.
Everywhere there are gnarled olive trees, citrus groves and heavenly smells.

So close to the railway for access to the towns along the line to Venice just over an hour away to the east. Visit Verona, Vicenza and Padua allowing a day for each.

In the other direction is Milan. Desenzano del Garda railway station is the gate way to all these destinations.

The lake has many lovely towns around its shores.
There is a good ferry service which serves the lake with many routes criss crossing the water.

Taxi boats are typically Italian and quite striking as they surge around in a speedy fashion.

Hilly and mountain walks are an attractive option. The northern aspect of the lake offers many lovely hotels located on the mountain sides with lake views.

Sermione has the remains of a splendid Roman villa at its northern point it is well worth a visit. Yes, there are tourist traps everywhere and hawkers from Africa selling cheap Chinese copies. It's popular but that is because it is all so winsome.

Lofoten

## Lofoten the beautiful

Rising like a wall appearing on the horizon.
Dark and foreboding in early dawn light
So early in the morning in later summer.

Separating into close knit islands
As the definition comes clearer in the light.
Lofty peaks with green sides to the water.

North of the Arctic Circle.
A village appears as our ship heaves to in the roads.
Lower the tenders we are going ashore.

Cod fish drying on frames everywhere.
An Ancient Trade
Harking back to the Hanseatic League.

An acquired taste they say!

We get on the bus.
Our guide is an Aussie lad from Perth
Far from home but loves Lofoton.

He regales us with poetry and song
As the bus rolls happily along
Crossing bridges and rounding rocky bends.

It is so warm, shirt sleeve weather sunny and bright
We arrive at our lunch venue. Fish of course.
Crisp and clear water as we walk the shore.

Heading back to the ship we imagine this place
In the grip of dark winter.
Our guide writes his poetry as snow and ice covers all.

Only a day but one no to be forgotten.

## Fees

Some fees are big but most are small
I'd like to find and smite them
Bigger fees have smaller fees upon their backs to bite em!

You pay!

They come in many shapes and forms
Money, seems to generate them
A percent of this a dob of that just as the mood will take them

Government, banks, and business
They just love to generate them
But universally 'tis true the public really hate 'em.

Fees may come and fees may go
But this is oh so true
Fees that serve no purpose make everybody blue.

So!

Keep on your guard with statements
On invoices and such
Then pounce on them and question them so very very much.

Expose all fees to ridicule
To the shame that they deserve
And maybe eliminate them but you need to keep your nerve

## Africa remembered

We spent some years in Africa Many years ago.
Memories, recalling them is a lovely treat.
Oh Africa, Oh Africa,
You so put us on our feet.

'Tis quite humbling to consider
Looking back down the years.
How easily we uprooted
Is it true we had few fears?

Like gold fish in bowl
That is often how we felt.
Guest workers
In a country hot enough to make us melt.

The expat community
They came from far and wide
A real United Nations
Temporarily together to reside.

Everywhere was beautiful
In Kenya where we were.
Mountain peaks and seaside
What a privilege to be sure.

Getting chased by elephants
And finding ticks upon our skin.
A little animal reminder
Of the bush we were just in.

Stuck in the mud I was
Down Naivasha way.
A working trip, I'm going home
Help from some locals, well I say!

Around by Lake Nakuru
Out for a ride one day.
Got chased by a secretary bird
When in the bushes she did stray. (For a pee)

Stupid, got stuck in the sand one trip
On Mombasa's northern side.
Arrives a bearded guy in 4 wheel drive
God's miracle to rescue us from the tide.

Up to the drive-in movies
A good treat after work.
Back to town for a veggie curry
Eaten with chapattis not a fork.

Afternoon tea with the Sheldrick's
At Tsavo Park also after work.
Sipping earl grey tea when,
A Kudu stole my biscuit and made everybody smirk.

(Tsavo National Park - David Sheldrick Chief Warden. Kudu - antelope with long twisted horns, big as a donkey.)

Getting sick in the Company plane
Following the H.T. line searching for a fault
Flying so slow it's wallowing,
Oh, my tummy, it's assault!

Africa, Oh Africa A lifetime ago

## Twist and turn in bed

It used to be quite easy
Getting comfortable in bed.
But now I find it difficult
My legs they feel like lead.

An itch can feel like murder
As I attempt to scratch it.
Sometimes I have to ask for
Assistance to dispatch it.

So thanks to all my helpers.
I hope you understand
How very much I appreciate it
When you lend me a hand.

**I got a new speaker thingy**

I'm lying here listening to my Bose
Listening
As it goes.

The Shadows they sound really great.
But I have turn the volume down
When the time it gets too late.

The dear old tranny never sounded quite so good.
Hank Marvin sounds so neat
His trusty Stratocaster twanging like it should.

It's really small this speaker thing, that is the truth
Small neat and beautiful
And running on Bluetooth.

## It's cold up North in Norway

One day I went to North Cape
As North as North can be

High cliffs facing outward
Across the windy Arctic sea

Inside the shop was warm and nice
Spray through the glass to see

But go outside and you will find
You're cut off at the knee.

I could not make it to the fence
I had to turn and flee.

So I found a very pleasant view
And sat and had some tea.

North Cape from the sea

## Friends

What can I say?
What can be said?
The beauty of friends.
It comes to this
So valuable it is.

To be so rich
It's blessing rare
The beauty of friends.
It comes to this
So valuable it is.

So my friends
Wherever you are
How beautiful you be
So it comes to this
So beautiful to me.

## To Hospital for my Infusion

I have to have infusions
I have one every other week.
I turn up of a lunch time.
So my immunity gets a tweak.

I have so much fun you see
It really is a sin.
Till the bloody nurse arrives
To stick the bloody catheter in.

Once that is over
I can lay back and relax.
I get to have a little chat
And eat some scrummy snacks.

Then it is all over
And I get this urge to roam,
So I call the local taxi man
And high tail it for home.

## Pumpkin Soup

Now I don't like pumpkin much
Strangely to relate.
Is that some pumpkin soup I see?
Give me another plate.

I don't know if it's cheap or not?
We get it fairly often.
We get some toast to go along
But, please let the butter soften!

We sit around the table
Wheelchairs all akimber (various angles)
All of us got gammy arms
So spreading butter is a bit difficult
(Sorry caught for a rhyme there)

We like the ham and pea as well
And spud and leeks not bad.
Good job we likes the pumpkin though
Or else we'd be quite sad.

## Miss Littleton

Fourteen and in love!
Hate English but love the teacher.
Must be her first job
I'm smitten.

Probably has five years on me
Sit behind on the bus going home.
We chat
I'm smitten some more.

I did well that year
In English I mean.
Ah!
Deary, deary me!

We all gather round
On the sports field.
She is leaving.
Getting married to a Mr Brown.

Not me!

## Saturday Morning Pictures

At the local Odeon
Theatre is crowded
The noise is deafening.

The manager tries to get us quiet.
We go silent when says.
No silence
No movies.

I'm there with Deidre, Sue and Bill.
We have been going together for three weeks
Summer liaisons
Doesn't last.

We are only eleven
Have juice one day
At Sue's house
Making necklaces with beads.

Cartoon's and Superman on the bill
Summer is soon over
The holiday is done
Nice to remember cos we had some fun.

## Embarrassing Day at the Races

When I was eleven at the school sports
I won rather more than my fair share of loot
100 yards
High jump
Long jump
And relay.
Comments behind hands
From mums on the bus.
Going home. My arms full.

## Mountain In The Sky

Flying past I spot it
Out of the left window
As we fly west.

Floating
Seemingly
Above the clouds.

Rising out of the plain
All alone
Majestic!

The disconnected summit
Covered in snow
In equatorial Africa.

## Too Many Paper Rounds

Dad passed away.
Mum decides to take us to Cornwall.
Uncle Pip is going to drive us down
I need money quick.

Local shops need paper boys
so many regulars away.
I offer.
Five rounds a day in the hol's

Three mornings
Two afternoons
One week!
Made two pounds ten.

It rained all week
And I got toothache
We stay four days
Then Pip takes us home.

**Perving the girls at 5**

Well would you believe it
Naughty little muse's
Watch the girls a skipping
Hoping for some views's

A bunch of us at infants!

East African Airways Booper!

We had an extra week
On Mahe Island Seychelles
Cos EAA cancelled the weekly flight.

Then going home following week.
The plane overflew
Mombassa airport where we were bound.

Meaning we landed at Nairobi
A long way from home!
Not to worry all in hand.

So, the air hostie took charge
Sped us through immigration
Sans luggage in no time flat.

Back on the plane
In first class no less
No time for booze.

I my suggestion
Pilots do short field take off
We are in a VC10. Wow!

We land at Mombassa
Only a caretaker in charge
A lonely cab waiting for us.

Home at last!

## Football

The objective:

Rugby league

To get rid of the ball before one or more big hunks grind your face into the mud!

Rugby union

To get rid of the ball before one or more big hunks grind your face into the mud while half your own team pile on top!

Soccer

To control the ball with your feet until some big hunk sticks his leg close enough to yours so that you can attempt to fly over it and land with a grimace on your face for all to see!

Grid iron

To hide the ball while all the big hunks bash the living daylights out of each other!

Australian rules

Big hunks trying to fly in skimpy shorts, catch the ball and land in one piece with manhood intact. The ladies love it!

Irish football

Impossible to make out the objective!

Cricket

What the big hunks do in the summer while attempting to be gentlemen□. Bears absolutely no resemblance to football. Takes a while to get to the objective.

## The Men's Shed

I love to go to Men's Shed
I go to have some fun.
Meeting with the others
For coffee, tea and bun.

I used to love to make stuff
But I can't do no more.
So I just goes for fun and fellowship
Where I can exercise my jaw.

We come together from all around
To meet up down the shed.
Gives me something to live for
Helps me get out of bed.

Clontarf community Men's Shed

## Gluten Free in France

Down in South West France
A place they call Dordogne.
Chateau littered everywhere
Some are not well known.

Looking for a place we were
That served up gluten free
Went to say with Kev and Bill
In a chateau, so lovely!

Château Villars, perfect
A beautiful place to stay.
Watched a tractor mow the grass
Giving birth to hay.

So many towns and villages
Scattered roundabout.
Full of history and such
A packed lunch to go out.

Brantome is my favorite
Best on market day.
Park down by the river
A lunch time place to stay.

Nontron and Perigueux
Are towns not very far away
St Jean on the river Cole.
Complete with square and a cafe.

Go for a walk to Puyguilhem
Up a one kilometer track
Visit a splendid castle
You could not call a shack.

The Château de Villars what a place to stay!

## Centerlink

I think it's amazing
In this modern age
That contacts made so difficult
That why I write this page.

One hour on the telephone
And that is if you are lucky.
Have they not heard of "call back"
It makes me get "up-chucky".

Mygov should be easy
Truth is it don't compute.
Cannot send an email
Menu's don't have the route.

So, here I sits unhappy
Wondering what to do.
I just feel frustrated
Do you feel that way too?

The staff they are amazing
So patient, nice and kind.
It's the Mandarin's above em
What's left us all behind.

So to politicians all
Whatever is your hue.
Sort out bloody Centrelink
Whatever you can do!

## The Three Stage Rocket Saga

Guy Fawkes Night is November the 5th in the UK. Fireworks, yahoo! To the teenager this is a time for wonder and experimentation. My best friend at that time (the year 1960) was Anthony Roberts. He'd been my best friend at school but by the time of this story - the Great Three Stage Rocket Project - we had both left.

Anthony lived in a large house that backed on to the Reigate County School for Girls. Sputniks and all things space were big news, so Anthony and I collaborated on our own project, pooling our funds to buy three sky rockets. One big monster costing half a crown, a shilling one, one for three pence and three bangers for one penny each of the old variety money. These we set about adapting. We removed the pod of the top of the big one and similarly the next size down. We set the contents aside for other later experiments. The big one was four foot high including the stick; the next size somewhat shorter. The three penny one had no pod with stars but we thought we should add a small one made of thin card with just a few of the stars and some gun powder inside. We did not know how far our magnificent beast would fly and we wanted to be able to see the final point of travel under power.

We sellotaped the second stage complete with stick to the primary stage and put the contents of one of the penny bangers in between together with one of the stars. These stars were like small pieces of hard gun powder with metal filings embedded. We did this to cause the used first stage to ignite the second stage and blow the first stage free having done its work. We hoped that the separation would be clean and the single star would give us an indication of this. The top stage was similarly mounted on the second stage to finish off the three stage rocket. The whole new assembly was just slightly heavier than the original largest rocket complete with its

original pod of stars so we hoped for good things.
The scene now moved from the assembly line in Anthony's bedroom to the end of the large garden where we had set up a launch facility consisting of a length of $\frac{3}{4}$ inch metal electric conduit hammered into the ground. We wanted our project to fly mostly upwards like the rockets on the news but we gave the launch facility a slightly eastern cant of somewhere about 5 degrees as we did not want the thing to go up and come down on our heads and we thought it likely that this arrangement would send our pride and joy in a predictable direction.
Well, NASA has had its share of failures but I proudly report that it should have consulted with us cos our little effort performed magnificently. I tell you it was majestic! On lighting the blue touch paper and retreating the recommended distance across the rose beds, we were rewarded with a great whoosh as the assemblage lifted off and headed high and true in the assigned direction. There was a pleasing pop and a bright green star appeared while the second stage continued skywards and down range. A second pop and another star this time a red one. The last stage being much smaller lasted only a couple of seconds but it was by this time travelling faster than any three penny rocket had ever achieved. Pop! But too far away down range for us to hear, maybe even as far as the boys Grammar School a mile and a half away, five stars appeared. Wow! We chose to make the flight at dusk. How high did it get? Well my estimate is well over five hundred feet. There was a pleasing contrail left in the sky.

Chris Brown (from Father Browns Stories 2017)

## The Upgrade

They sent another upgrade mum
I bet it turns out bad.
They change the stuff we're used to
I makes my tummy sad.

It comes up on me IPad
It comes up on me phone.
It drives me mad how often
It causes me to moan.

Sometimes they really stuff it up
It causes me to cringe.
Yet more upgrades come along
They make me want to whinge.

Now all you nerdy programmers
We know you love your job
But why not get it right just once
Not try to make us sob.

The learning curve Its long you know
The bigger software grows.
Life is all to short you know
So why add to our woes.

## On The News (Entebbe Raid)

Woke up to the sound
Of planes flying low!
Where is it they have come from?
Where is it they will go?

We found out in the morning
Cos it was on the news.
A daring rescue had been performed
Saving passengers by the Jews.

## Racing cars

Back in the 1950's
Dinky toys were all the rage.
I collected racing cars
About 10 years of age

Maserati, Ferrari and Alpha
And many more beside.
Lovingly in a shoe box
I kept at my bed side.

At school we had a race track
Dug on a slope with a stick.
We made it fast and beautiful
Once we had learned the trick.

My fastest was the Vanwall
That was a British make
Stirling Moss once drove one
I drove mine down our muddy snake.

The poor Vanwall got quite battered
Speeding down the hill.
But it made me the winner
It gave me such a thrill.

I wonder where they all went
I don't have them today.
Wrapped up in their tissues
Ready for next time to play.

THE
Vanwall

## Lamu

A sweet little island
On the North Kenya coast
Famous in Africa
A Muslim pilgrimage site.

Mostly sand and coconut trees
Historical site
Famous for its doors
No cars allowed.

Was there before the monsoon
Business was all done
Started to rain after breakfast
Pilot said time to go.

Over the water to the strip
In a dhow, it's pelting.
The strip is awash already
Power up we are off.

The Briton Norman islander
Hops from puddle to puddle
Up and away
As the bush scrapes by below.

Lamu rained in now for months.

Views of Lamu Island
Beach Hotel, Town Front
and Fishing Dhows

## Venice.

Gliding over the water
Near to sunset.
Rising out the shimmer
Beauty appears to rise.

A golden city
Floating on a dark sea
The buildings float up
They take shape.

We land at St Marks
Walking past icons
We plunge into the alleyways
No idea which direction.

Then down some steps
We enter a cafe place
Wine and opera
A Musicanty.

It is dark when we finish
Back through the gloom
Our gorgeous taxi boat awaits
Whisking us away under a silver moon.

## The Back Road in the Rift Valley

Heading back home
Along the valley of the great Rift.
I take a seldom used road
Driving a land Cruiser.

Over the back of Longanot volcano
Up the western escarpment.
Get out of the car at a high spot.
Walk a little way through the bush.

This is a bit silly me thinks
Miles from anywhere.
Not my country anything lurks
I sit on the edge looking down.

It stretches away north.
Lake Elimantita in the distance
It shimmers in the sun.
I make my way back.

A disturbed antelope startles me
Leaps up and bounds away
Cannot see what sort.
Back safely at the truck.

Soon enough I rejoin the main road
Heading along the familiar path
It takes me home for tea.
It was worth the risk.

## New Zealand Fjords

Floating in the lap of luxury
The boat slides between rock walls.
Gliding across the ebony water
Past cascading waterfalls.

Snow on the peaks glistens
We keep watchful eye for seals
We're a long way from anywhere
At least that's how it feels.

At the end in Milford Sound
Down past Mytre Peak.
Just room to turn the ship around
We head back to the deep.

Down the coast a little way
We turn and head back in
Running right through Doubtful Sound
Missing this would be a sin.

Dusky Sound starts off the same
Then islands pass in the even.
As we emerge and round the cape
And Head up to Dunedin.

**As I look out my window**

My bed is by the window
Trees and houses opposite.
Our unit is just up the road
Which is rather apposite

I can get there swiftly and with style
Riding my electrical chariot
Fast enough to make me smile.

Shall I go the long way
By the Bally River along the path?
Or chance it on the roadway
Dodging motors for a laugh?

So lying here I contemplate a while
What is it that I shall do?
Be done swiftly and with style.

Not sure changing the metre works?

## Not Enough Sockets

I am happy with my room
I'm a happy little sprocket
I got so much computer stuff
I need another socket!

## How Much Is Your Stuff Worth

We gotta move
There really is no choice.
The prospect is alarming
It upsets our equipoise.

But there is a problem
As if that weren't enough.
The house is full to burstin'
We just have so much stuff!

What to get rid of
What should we keep?
A topic of conversation
It prevents us getting sleep.

Of course there is the op shop
And then the garage sale.
Just the thought drives us nuts
We are getting rather pale.

Then there is the value?
That comes into it.
In our eyes it is still worth
What we shucked out for it!

At last it's all gone
Anyway nearly all
We are now so tired
It's into bed we fall.

Had to accept our treasure
Was not worth that much.
There's a lesson in there somewhere
We crammed too much in our hutch.

## Pizzas

I'm coming home for pizza dear
I like them gluten free
With lots a bits and pieces
On the top for me to see.

I help chop up the toppings
Laying on the cheese
With olives, and other flavorings
Made quickly and with ease.

Twelve minuets in the oven
At 180 degrees
The cheese gets to melting
And the sight it starts to please.

Then it's time to cut them up
Arrange them on the plate
I'm now quite full and satisfied
Tonight bed won't be late.

## The beauty of holiness

Take time to be holy they say
Is this something I can do?
Or am I just a basket case
And could you be one too?

Trying harder is a game
And we all can get sucked in
It's hard to get the picture
When I'm smothered up in sin.

So what is the reality?
This condition that I'm in?
Thank God there is an answer
I need not be taken in.

Praise God there is good news
It's there for everyone.
Jesus, he came to save us
The deed has all been done.

So I can live and be set free
It's true for you as well.
The prison door is open
So why still live in your cell.

The Father has good things for you
So why not opt right in.
Living in the moment
It's exciting and we win.

## Wednesday is bacon sarny day

What is this all covered with ally foil?
Oh my! It's my bacon sarny kit.
My mouth waters.
It and I are destined for close quarters.

First I remove excessive fat.
Because I'm a Jack Sprat.
I dorb the bread in hot mustard.
Not too much it is not custard!

I like it slightly crispy,
Not often that I get it.
But I like it anyway, sometimes even Monday,
Any day that's bacon day is definitely a funday.

## Going to Lunch at Sam's

Poor as church mice we are.
Just about able to fork out two shillings each.
For lunch on a Saturday at Sam's
The transport cafe on the Gatwick roundabout.

Famous for speed of delivery it is.
Friend Ian's dad runs the joint.
Guesses what people will order.
Usually he is right.

Fish chips and peas.
Sausage chips and peas.
Pie chips and peas.
Steak chips and peas.

All served swiftly with a wad of bread
And a large mug of tea - well stewed.
After's is six pence extra.
On a good day we indulge.

We walk back home replete.
Maybe one day we will frequent
A proper restaurant.
Yes that would be nice.

But praise God for Sam's
It keeps the Lorries rolling.
It keeps the home fires burning.
Next week we'll be returning - to Sam's.

## Dinner at Kilravock Castle

Kilravock Castle close to Culloden Moor.
On holiday in the Highlands
We have an invitation to dinner
From Elizabeth Rose the Laird.

Over five hundred years old
Steeped in history.
Dinner is served in the hall
High up in the tower.

Later we enjoy some singing
Along with other guests in the salon.
The Castle is now a Christian guest house.
We enjoy the privilege.

Elizabeth arranged for our accommodation.
With quiet Sandy and his good wife
Who prefaced much conversation with the expression
Sandy says!

We attend the local Church of Scotland service.
The pulpit is high up the wall.
Well above any contradiction!
The offering is collected using boxes on poles.

In the middle of summer it never gets dark.
Just a twilight.
The cows are munching in the field
In the midnight glow.

## Who do we know who has a Jag?

Sunday afternoon nap time.
Snoozing in the bedroom at the front.

There is a revving engine outside
It disturbs the peace, who thus disturbs?

I peer out the curtained window
Who do we know with a Jag E type love?

No one she replies sweetly.
Well we do now cos Pam's just getting out of one.

At the front door Pam mutters
On your best behavior brother this might be him!

Enter John, with Aussie accent.
Dentist cashing in on NHS. Doing well apparently.

There is a wedding fairly soon.
Swank hotel in London.

Parking boy sniffs at my humble car.
Ah! well humble it may be but it is ours.

## Rambling in Surrey

Saturday morning and it is raining a little
More a mist really.
We gather at the start point
A bridal track heading into the countryside.

We are a mixed group of teens
We have an ordinance survey map
We come to a style over a fence
It leads into a wheat field.

Following the path we skirt the paddock
Keeping the code we close gates as we pass.
Another style leads us into the woods.
The bluebells are out carpeting the ground.

We find a stout oak tree with low branches
Great for climbing around.
Through the woods we enter a church yard
Wandering among the headstones.

Up the road into a pretty village
We stop to buy drinks at the shop.
It is lunch time and the sun has warmed up
So we find the village green and eat.

One remarks it is the longest village in the world
It has two pubs, one each end.
The "The Rising Sun" and "The Full Moon".
That makes strange sense.

Someone brought a football
The pitch still has its goal posts.
Picking up sides the game is on.
No one minds about the score much.

It is time to head back.
Consulting the map we agree which way.
We skirt the airport boundary.
Tired but happy we breakup and head home.

Very old photos

## Lee St Church

A tin shed on a byway
Not very prepossessing.
A place of God's appointment
Ready with a blessing.

For a lonely kid whose lost his dad?
He finds a new formed group of boys.
He needs new friends to join with
So there's no need of some ploys.

It all seems very simple looking back
A Gospel of redemption
Good news
Good news

## We Got the Builders In

Woke up this morning
To such an awful din.
The peace it has been shattered
We got the builders in!

The grinding and the drilling
The thumping on the roof of tin.
Yep, you may have guessed it
We got the builders in!

They're fitting in the kitchen
The swearing it's a sin.
The pushing and the shoving
Yes, we got the builders in!

They say it will be lovely
We'll break out in a grin.
But for now we're putting up with it
Cos' we got the builders in.

## Breakfast at Norfolk Hotel Nairobi

A new job far away in Africa.
Flying in late quite at night
Tom toms beating give us a fright
We wake up to the morning light.

Getting up it's time for eats.
In the mood we look for food
Looking to see if the coffee's brewed
Or making sure the tea's not stewed.

Amazing sight before our eyes.
A smorgasbord immense to see
So much food is it all for me?
In the Norfolk Hotel it's so good to be.

Never seen so much before
What a view, it's really neat
Could we have fallen on our feet?
This is going to be hard to beat.

## God looks on the heart which is on the inside

Am I building a picture to hide behind?
What will people think?
Where do I hide?
Hiding behind my hands
You can't see me!

God sees me, no ifs no buts.
The Holy one sees the inside.
He loves me on the inside.
I'm not sure He even likes the outside.
The outside which I build.

God hates sin, why?
Because it messes up what He loves.
God is not put off by sin.
He habitually forgives.
He builds, restores, and fixes up.

I try to formulate the view.
Map out the plan. A box for God!
But God laughs at our efforts.
Building walls of fake good news.
For God looks on the inside.

It's a warfare.
Warfare is messy.
It's hard to tell.
Progress it's hard to measure.
Love does not keep score.

This is not all there is.
There is a Kingdom to Come!
A New Heaven and a New Earth.
A new morning, real Good News.
Here is hope. We all need!

## The Eggs are Hard

In Queensland Aged Care facilities all eggs must have hard yokes. It's the Law apparently.

Oh dear, just look into my poor fate
Poached and very hard upon my plate.
I'd like them quite soft
But my knife it bounced of
So they are not something I ate.

There may be salmonella they say though it is rare and can be avoided.
Unlike the general public I get no choice!

## Poem about Jock

A young handsome fellow named a Jock
Liked to get out and about in a frock.
Not wanting to be left in the lurch
He upped and went into the Church
Now he joins people up in wedlock.

## Prayer Points

Do I reckon God is good?
Does He know what He is doing?
Is He always achieving His desires?
Can I tell where He is going?

God be good!

Even thinking that God is good
Do I truly believe He is able?
To achieve His desires
Even if many say "not do-able"?

Do I believe?

Is there a way of knowing?
Of knowing for sure what God Wants?
Where would you find out?
Would it, could it be among the fonts? (writings)

What does God want?

What will always be true?
Or is the right question, who?
Where do I rest my case?
Being sure He will see it all through.

What can I take for granted?

To a God who good, able and true
What would be offensive from His point of view?
To treat Him as a mere god
Is that what we could inadvertently do!

What would be too rude to pray?

What room is open?
For having a chat?
Should I feel free?
To say where I'm at?

Negotiating with God?

How to do it
What is the approach?
Who will assist me
I'm needing a coach.

Worship protects from error?

All things are possible.
With God I've heard say.
Has anything changed?
Or is this for today?

The miraculous

There's safety in numbers
I've heard people say.
Is that where the power
In praying could lay?

Power in numbers?

Are we out to impress
Is it the numbers that come?
Or are we present to be more
Accountable to some?

Let your words be just few.

Yes praying is perplexing
Let's not obfuscate
Approach it quite lightly
It's never too late.

In everything

## Working with Charlie

How blessed am I to be allotted Charlie Bourner.
I'm doing my apprentice time.
Six years with the South Eastern Electricity Board.
Charlie gets the big jobs. Good for me.

Charlie commands great respect.
A graduate of the Burma Railway.
Captured like so many in Singapore.
Nineteen years old. Survived.

Deacon of Horley Baptist Church.
Charlie helped me wire up Lee St Church.
A holiday job for me.
His advice so helpful.

Surely goodness and mercy shall follow me
All the days of my life.
Until we meet again Charlie
See ya soon.

## Your Call Is Important To Us

Oh yes your call is important to us
We wanted you all to know.
So we tacked this message on
That our concern would be on show!

Of course we are rather busy
Or we could even be asleep.
How would you know in either case?
Please leave a message after the beep.

We are so thankful for your call
Yes we really mean it.
We look forward to being of service
We want you to believe it.

Don't waste your cash
Don't do your dash
Leave us a message
And then press hash.

## The young lady from Cheam

There was a young lady from Cheam
Who wanted to let off some steam.
There was some wild talk
That she'd blown her cork
But it's all in the mind it would seem.

There was a young lady from Cheam
Who woke up in a sweat from a dream
She'd visioned a hunk
Who was quite a spunk
But we won't dwell no more on that theme.

There was a young lady from Cheam
Who had a vibrating machine
I will tell your more
It was a mechanical saw
I caught you out there, what a scream!

Cheam - A Village not far from Epsom horse race track South West London.

## Dyslexic

I am a dyslexic
There are gaps within my brain
Is there a dyslexic anonymous?
Where I could go and train?

I often Wright notes too myself
To save myself embarrassment.
Unfortunately I can't read them
Which really is an harassment.

Computers are a real boon
Spelling checkers are a gift.
As I can always blame them
Instead of getting miffed.

The English language is at fault
There is a problem their
They're is no way to work it out
I do not think it fare.

Oh what is to become of me?
It's been a life long struggle
Will somebody help me out?
When I get in a muddle.

Some people laugh, but that's not fair
But what is one to do?
I suppose it runs in families
My sister had it too.

## The Story of Brunswick Green

Now there is a something just not to be seen
Never put blue next to Brunswick Green.

It's just pure seventies matt or with sheen
Referring of course to Brunswick Green.

Once all the rage, it's now a has been
Paint it all over that Brunswick Green.

It had a mate that now causes a frown
It had a name too, it was called Mission Brown.

Is there a place that is somewhere mesne?
Could that be a place called Brunswick Green?

Mesne is a word that means in between.
So useful, it rhymes with Bruns-a-wick Green.

## Light Fingers

Parsons and Peas
And Leonard P Rees
They were solicitors of note

Their names are quite funny
They were in for the money
Trying to make a quick groat.

They gathered a stash
Of accumulated cash
A wheeze that could not fail

They gathered from clients
By handling the finance
But eventually they wound up in jail.

## Flying to Turkana

One day we flew in a little plane
Clear as a bell
There was no rain.

Good job too we would say
As where we went
Is very much a desert stay.

Lake Turkana is a lovely place
In North West Kenya.
Hot and dry and in your face.

The lake is huge as one could wish.
The Turkana live here
Catching enormous fish.

Ferguson's Gulf is where we land
We buzzed the lodge.
A Land Rover comes across the sand.

Night time and we launch a boat
Across the water quietly drift.
Where crocs look just like logs that float.

Fancying a swim, don't play the fool!
In the black darkness
We get into the pool.

Our stay is sadly rather short
We fly next day
To our home port.

Lake Turkana Nth West Kenya

**Once I owned a bubble car**

Yes, I once owned a bubble car
It was neither old nor new.
The one I had was coloured grey
Nicer if it had been coloured blue.

It was as long as it was wide
It really was quite small.
Somehow I got inside it
When over six feet tall.

One day out in the ice and snow
Approaching to a junction.
I did a complete 360
When the steering lost its function.

But I was sensible most times
Was not always doing twirls.
One day I tried to fill it up
That's, fill it up with girls!

Now it was not a chick magnet
Or anything like that
I did go courting in it though.
As a matter of a fact.

We went on down to Brighton
To buy my girl a ring.
When the big end gave out on me
Another expensive thing!

After fixing it 'twas time to go
The bubble had burst by then.
We pooled our cash together
And we bought a Standard 10.

So what was it my bubble car?
A BMW that's better!
Truly it was a Beamer
That's a BMW Isetta.

Registration No 6073 PO

BMW Isetta

Chris Brown - chris@brownsplace.id.au

www.ingramcontent.com/pod-product-compliance
Ingram Content Group UK Ltd.
Pitfield, Milton Keynes, MK11 3LW, UK
UKHW020235250726
13967UKWH00001B/388